surfacing

closing practices for creative writers

Emily Stoddard

for the writers of
the Hummingbird Sessions

with gratitude for the infinite
openings, closings, unknowns, and
in-betweens we wrote through
together

CONTENTS

How you
surface from
your writing time
can be just as
meaningful
as how you begin—

How do you mark the thresholds of your
creative practice as a writer?

What does the beginning of your writing
time usually look or feel like? What about
the ending?

What does it mean to enter and exit your
writing space?

To open and close a notebook?

So much emphasis is placed on beginnings:
the rituals and tools that help a writer
"get into" the work. The prompts that
loosen us up, playlists we curate for
inspiration, and so on.

The threshold IN to writing is one of the
most clearly marked and supported spots in
the process.

But the threshold OUT of writing practice
is less clear, less consistent, and (I
think) very underappreciated.

What insights do you miss if you "drop"
your writing and head out the door?

What momentum is lost when we skip a
thoughtful close to our practice?

What if a thoughtful closing is what
creates a feeling of continuity in our
practice?

Like a dancer removing their shoes or a
painter cleaning their brushes, how can
writers have a hands-on way of emerging
from practice?

I call this surfacing.

I think of my writing as a body of water:
I tend to dive deep, float away, respond to
invisible currents and lose sight of the
shore. Immersion is the joy of writing for
me... but it makes it difficult to come up
for air, leave my writing space, and
continue my day in the much more land-
locked, linear, and everyday world.

THE PRACTICE OF SURFACING:

* marks the threshold / celebrates practice.

* prepares a writer for departure / eases the
transition from the creative space to the
everyday space.

* captures insights (results of practice)
that might otherwise be missed / observes
what you're learning as a writer, at a moment
when your awareness is primed.

* creates a continuity of practice / leaves an
opening for a thoughtful return next time.

* builds momentum as you unearth memories
and raw material / helps identify through-
lines as they emerge.

* gives nonlinear, neurodivergent writers a
way to "land" after floating out in creative
work / provides a tether to come out of the
rabbit hole.

* guides the creative act from feeling like
luck, random inspiration, or abstract vibes to
a series of choices and experiments.

SURFACING is:

* for writers of any experience level.

* for projects in any form, genre, or
style.

* short and simple by design, usually
three to 10 minutes before you exit your
writing time.

* yours to make your own... find more
guidance at the end of this book.

A SIMPLE PRACTICE
TAKEN SERIOUSLY
IS MORE POWERFUL THAN
AN ELABORATE PROCESS
DONE TO EXHAUSTION

practicing with this book

The practice of surfacing from your writing time is simple on purpose.

It is not a system.

It is not a twenty-step process.

It is a practice.

Some writers may have an inner voice that says, "This is too simple. This feels too easy. Will this really do anything?"

When I started leading workshops, I learned how often writers are skeptical of simple practices. (I've been one of them.) Think of all the expensive retreats and elaborate drafting systems out there for writing. There's an unspoken insistence that because the creative process seems mystifying, it should be complicated in practice.

I keep learning how much the opposite is true.

Creativity loves a simple practice. Simple practices ignore gatekeepers, divert critics, and skip theatrics. Simplicity dares us to work with what we already have... a dare that I think Creativity loves to accept.

A simple practice taken seriously will always outwit an elaborate process done exhaustively.

So surfacing is a simple practice. It's yours to make your own, to take seriously or not. Here are ways I work with it:

<u>Use it whenever you write, no matter how long you write.</u> I developed this as part of the Hummingbird Sessions. Those were 15 minutes each, an experiment in generating deep attention on a small scale. Even though it was "just" 15 minutes of writing, I led us in a closing practice each time. It made the writing more of a ritual. It helped us transition back to our daily lives. Don't discount brief stints of writing. (Time gets overemphasized as a measure of "good" practice. A hummingbird is small, but her wings create infinity.)

<u>Try repeating a closing practice for a
week, a month, a whole project.</u> Especially
if you're interested in tracking progress
with a certain memory or material, or if
you're trying to get more skilled with a
certain technique.

<u>Make field notes.</u> Surfacing can be a
reflective and ephemeral exercise—just a
pause before you leave the work, with no
record of how you responded. But I find it
most helpful to jot down notes or
impressions. Sometimes these notes happen
in the margins of a draft, but usually I
put them in a notebook reserved for field
notes. For typing lengthier notes (or if
my brain is moving faster than my hand), I
use an app called DayOne. You can tag
notes as "surfacing" and/or with the
project name. I love how this builds
evidence of practice. When I'm feeling lost
in later revisions on a piece, I'll return
to earlier closing practice notes and find
a question or observation to get the work
flowing again.

THE PRACTICES

There are 70 closing practices in this book. They generally take three to 10 minutes each. For some, I've suggested specific times.

I numbered the practices in case you'd like to keep track of which ones you've used. If you work with one repeatedly, it can be interesting to notice how your responses change over time or vary from project to project.

1

For three minutes, write as many possible endings as you can for the starters below. I like to alternate them, repeating one after the other until I've filled a page (the words are... the process is.... the words are... the process is...):

The words are taking the shape of a...

The process is moving like a...

2

How did the timing of today's practice feel?

Was it too early in the day, too late, just right?

Was the pace quick and energizing, or challenging? Was it slow and steady? Or lagging?

(What are you noticing about your temperament as a writer, as it relates to time and pacing?)

3

Where do you feel eager or restless in your writing now?

How did that influence your practice today?

What's one way it pulled you deeper into the work?

What's one way it pushed you out of the work?

4

Find one line or sentence that refuses to hide or apologize for what it's trying to say. Write it on a fresh sheet of paper or in a journal for three minutes of closing attention.

What tone, mood, energy, or feeling is present in this line? How present was that tone in your writing today? In general?

How is this tone or mood helping you access the material (i.e., the idea or memory you're writing about)?

5

Which line, sentence, or paragraph is
here to remind you of something you
tend to forget?

Highlight or underline it in your
writing today. If any follow-up
thoughts come through as you surface
with it, jot those down in the margins
or in the spot where you keep your
field notes.

6

Which phrase felt the strangest or most
surprising to write today?

Did you resist it or receive it easily?

For five minutes, jot down any
reactions you have to this phrase.
Invent a list of questions you have for
it or about it.

Let any question come through and give
it a space to land, even if you don't
understand what it means yet.

Questions like this are a way to catch
what's just beginning to stir in the
writing. And they're good placeholders
for returning to the material later.

7

Find a sentence or image in the writing today that comes from a place, feeling, or person you visit when no one is watching.

Rewrite the sentence or image on a piece of paper to carry out with you.

8

Which memory, idea, character, or moment in the writing is challenging your expectations for or understanding of this material?

You don't have to know all the reasons why... just observe which part it is. Jot down three things you know, imagine, or feel about it before leaving the page today.

9

Find three lines or sentences that
repeat or echo each other.

Maybe they repeat an idea, a specific
word, an image, or a sound.

Pull the lines out on a separate page
and make some brief notes:

What element is repeating?

Does it point to a larger pattern in
this piece of writing or your body of
work?

What's one way you'd like to experiment
with this pattern more directly? Leave
yourself a "what if I tried..." question
for when you return to this writing.

10

Who or what was your ally for practice today? What got you to the page and helped you stay with it?

Who or what was your adversary? What got in the way, made noise, or tried to distract?

You don't have to solve the tension between these two before you go. It's enough to make note of their presence, taking notes on any observations that show up as you name them.

11

Find a line that feels whole. Maybe a line that feels strong, a line that knows what it wants, or a line that really takes up all the space you have in your voice right now.

Pull this line out and write it on a separate slip of paper for yourself.

In the week ahead, as you feel uncertainty or curiosity, come back to this line. Journal with it as your starter for a few minutes, or maybe just repeat it yourself, to reconnect with the space it's making.

12

Find a page, stanza, or scene that
feels like it might have been written
by your future self... the writer you
are becoming.

What qualities, word choices, or moods
are present in this writing?

For two minutes, make a list of
characteristics you notice. (There are
no wrong possibilities, no details that
are too much or too little on a list
like this.)

13

Find a line that feels like it's fishing for something, that's waiting for something to catch, that's trying to hook on to something more.

What are you or a character longing for in this writing?

What are you longing for in your creative practice?

How did you try to bring it closer today?

14

When you imagine completing this project or piece of writing, what does the release look like? Feel like?

In this moment, as you surface from the work, does this feel like a project you want to release sooner, later, or not at all?

There are no wrong answers, and the answer might change over time. For today, before you go, observe what "release" means to this writing.

15

Which phrase or sentence is declaring
something it knows, refusing to hide a
feeling, or even shouting for
attention?

What if this became the working title
of this draft or a new project?

16

For three minutes, make a list of different ways a writer can tell if the work is done.

You can try these starters:

I'll know the writing is done when...

The writer feels finished when...

The process might be complete when...

17

What feels quiet, silent, or absent in
your writing today? Maybe it's
something that's gone unsaid. Maybe it's
a memory that's feeling reserved or
unspoken, like a shadow just behind the
writing. Find one image or line from
that space. No need to provoke this
line or ask why it's being quiet. It's
enough to notice that it showed up.

If it calls to you, return to some of
your other recent writing and find
three more lines that seem to come
from this space. Bring the lines
together in a small, rough poem—again,
not to provoke them, but just to hold
a little space for this side of your
voice as you leave the work.

18

Find one sentence that might be telling a joke. This could be overtly, as in a line that's funny in some way. Or it could be subtle, like a line that's not taking itself too seriously, or a line that makes a play on words. Pull this sentence out and write three more in its style, tone, or mood... just to observe the posture a little more and try it on.

Take a couple minutes for field notes: How does this tone or style feel to you? What is it doing for the writing that other styles haven't? Is this an area you're developing consciously in your practice, or is this sentence a surprise?

19

What word or sentence was showing you something new today? A new angle on an idea, a new technique, a new texture or tone in your voice, a new sound... ??

What makes this new or different? Do you want to carry it out of practice as an area for more exploration (on the page, in your reading, etc.)?

20

Find the riskiest, weirdest, or most courageous line or sentence.

Note where it falls in the piece. How did it emerge in that spot? How did you write toward it?

How does its placement in the writing feel? What if it was at the beginning? What if it was at the end?

Jot down your reactions to those possibilities. This could be a place to begin next time, and it may point to an aspect of the material that's trying to break loose or expand.

21

Underline, highlight, or note the strongest moment/phrase/word on each page or in each stanza.

If you're able, say each one out loud to yourself. Alternatively, you could rewrite each one on a separate sheet of paper, to see them together as a distinct group.

If these were the only things you had written today, what would they say is most important right now?

22

Where did you feel bored today?

What are some words or feelings you associate with boredom?

What if boredom had more space, more permission to play in your flow? To blur your attention?

How does boredom change your expectations for yourself as a writer? (And is that really a bad thing?)

23

Find a spot where you ruminated in the writing or a character wondered about something.

Rewrite this as 10 different questions, starting with the words HOW or WHAT IF. Try to make each question weirder or more direct than the last.

Circle the question that you love or hate the most. Leave it as an opening to continue the writing next time.

24

What are you celebrating about your writing or creative practice now?

What is something you have, know, or feel now, after having written, that you didn't have, know, or feel before you wrote today?

25

What is your writing teaching you to
remember?

(In one sentence, how is it doing
that?)

What is your writing teaching you to
forget?

(In one sentence, how is it doing
that?)

26

What's one concrete detail or object
that emerged in the writing today?

How might you <u>obsess</u> over this detail
or object a little more? Write one more
line or sentence for it before you go.

What could you <u>profess</u> about it? Do
you love it? Do you hate it?

Or is it possible it has something to
<u>confess</u>? What does it know that you,
your speaker, or a character do not
know yet?

27

Which line felt most satisfying to write, revise, or tinker with today?

Any definition of satisfying works, and this might be a chance to reflect on what satisfaction means to your practice. Which line filled the well for you? Which one felt good to write— maybe the words themselves just feel good to put on the page? Or maybe it's satisfying in sound or feeling? Or maybe it was rewarding to return to a particular memory?

As you go deeper in your writing, how are small choices, one line at a time, sustaining the work or satisfying you?

28

Where do you feel your writing asking you to give a little more, stay a little longer, wish a little bigger? What's one specific, generous response you could offer?

It's tempting to think of time as the main thing we can give our practice. In what other ways are you being generous now, or might you be generous?

29

Find a paragraph or stanza that thinks
it knows more than you do. Sometimes
these can be humorous lines, almost
like the writing is winking or smirking
at us. Sometimes the lines or phrasing
can feel precocious or provocative.

Take note of who the speaker is in this
moment. What does their voice sound
like? What attitude or tone do you
notice?

What perspective is coming through, and
how does that seem to be influencing
the material so far? Jot down three
notes about this voice and its
perspective.

30

What's the <u>smallest</u>, most <u>specific</u>,
almost <u>absurdly particular</u> thing your
writing wants or needs right now?

There is no such thing as

a wrong answer

or

a selfish answer

or

a foolish answer

so try an honest answer.

31

What writing advice did you ignore today?

How did it free you up to write? How did it change your relationship to the work, for better or worse, in big or small ways?

32

Find a spot in the writing where something changed. It could be as subtle as someone moving to another room or as big as a life decision being made.

How did you stay with this moment, as a writer and within the material? Did you make conscious choices about this scene or memory, or did it emerge organically?

(What's one way you can tell when you're really "in it" and inhabiting a moment, scene, or memory as you write?)

33

Find one line that reminds you of why
you write at all.

For one minute, make a list of reasons
why. There are no wrong answers.
Today's answers might be different than
tomorrow's, and that's okay.

34

As you surface from practice, spend a few more moments with the speaker in today's writing.

What mood, energy, or opinion was coming through most clearly for them today? If you are the speaker, try imagining yourself as a character to get some distance here.

For two minutes, make a list of things they are NOT saying or doing.

If any observations or questions pop up as you make the list, jot them down in a margin or write a quick field note.

35

What repeats in your writing, either in
the material itself or your process?
What do you do over and over? What do
you write about over and over?

Repetition can be a creative force:

SUBCONSCIOUSLY (your instincts)
Revealing a pattern or symbolism that's
potentially meaningful to the story

CONSCIOUSLY (your creative choices)
Emphasizing themes, adding weight and
energy, amplifying what can't be ignored

What is one repetition you sense you're
working with consciously now?

36

What's one way you companioned
yourself today?

Did you notice your breath? Stretch
your fingers? Calm a worried inner
critic?

How did you give yourself what you
needed to stay with the page and in
your practice? Is this the seed of a
ritual you could repeat next time?

37

Where did you sense yourself THINKING
through the writing today?

Where did you sense yourself FEELING
in the writing today?

Can you find a line that speaks to
each question?

What do these lines have in common?

Which orientation (thinking or feeling)
seems to be most helpful or surprising
as you work with this material?

38

Find an <u>edge</u> in your writing today: a line or sentence that reached for an idea, mood, truth, or belief that's different from the rest of the writing.

Where did the words get a little wild or sideways, even uncomfortable?

Offer this edge three minutes of attention. Make a list of any words, questions, or phrases it sparks for you. I like to think of this as shaking everything out of an unusual sentence before I go... these lines often have more to say, and sometimes they haunt us after we've left the page. This exercise is a way to release the work now and leave some possibilities for the next time you write.

39

What's one thing you know or want for
your writing today that would surprise
the writer you were three years ago?

40

What's the smallest detail that appeared in the writing today?

Maybe it's small in scale, like a coat button.

Maybe it's small in time or feeling, like a glance.

Write with or about this small detail for three more minutes, as if it's the most important thing that happened in the writing today.

41

Find one honest feeling or idea that came through in the writing today.

What words are attached to it? How have you given it a name on the page?

Resist any urge to censor or soften it now. This is not about revision.

Jot down at least five other possible names for this idea or feeling. (What images do you associate with it? What colors or sounds?)

What kind of RANGE do you notice in these associations? Do you sense your writing opening up today, or is it honing in?

42

What space is your speaker, narrator, or main character holding today?

Is the voice on the page close, active, involved?

Is it removed, observant, distant?

How are you playing with space, distance, and closeness in your writing now? Is it similar to or different from how you've worked with space in the past?

43

What if your body of creative work
took the shape of a body of water?

What's at the shore, reaching you?
What do you KNOW?

What's farther out and coming in, like
a wave? What do you SENSE?

Where's the undertow? What do you
QUESTION or DOUBT?

44

Where do you feel a little foolish in your practice today? A little out of your depth? Even naïve or short on wisdom?

No need to judge it. It's not a bad thing! Our inner fools can be the caretakers of new and needed possibilities. Write yours a letter for three minutes as you exit your writing. Consider making a promise.

45

Where do you notice a "give and take"
in your writing now?

Where do you dive in freely?

Where do you hold back?

Bring some curiosity. Why might this
be? How does it create tension... or
point to a detail you might be
resisting?

Where are you figuring out how to give
more as a writer?

46

Find a paragraph, stanza, or scene that feels especially knotted.

A place where things get tight or complicated, for better or worse. Maybe a comment or a truth that's not easily taken back or undone.

Meet this with some distance as your writer-artist-self (especially if it's material you've lived): what do you admire in the knot? What creative choices, techniques, or skills helped the knot appear in this writing?

47

What if you took a line, sentence, scene, or stanza less seriously? Return to one that feels heavy, murky, or tense.

Invent one thing the speaker could do, think, feel, or say that's irreverent. Maybe even bizarre. Something that breaks the rules of what they "should" be doing, thinking, feeling, or saying.

How does irreverence show up in your practice (or not)?

48

Where did you catch yourself trying something new today? Where did you sense you were in the process of discovering something?

Make note of the material you were working with, the tone or style of the writing (e.g., loose or tight? descriptive or distanced?), and how it felt to work with it.

Try underlining or highlighting some of your favorite lines from this space of discovery. What's the first thing you'd like to try with them the next time you write?

49

Where did you notice a long thought,
event, or action in the writing today?

LONG, as in:

lasting (in memory)
tall or wide (in space)
extended (in time)
remote (in distance)
deep (in feeling)

What kind of long is it today?

What might this signal for where you're
at with this material, or what you're
learning as a writer?

50

RECIPE FOR A ROUGH POEM

Making a found poem by picking lines
or phrases from your writing (even if
you're not a poet) can be a way to
honor the work. Don't worry about
making sense... meet each prompt for
each line as its own possibility, and
then read your found poem as a whole.

1. a line with a hope or a want
2. a line that tells the truth
3. a line that refers to a color,
   place, or sound
4. a line that feels especially raw or
   weird
5. a line that knows or remembers
   something important

51

QUESTIONS can be side doors, hidden passageways. Questions stir up the water of what we think we know. Questions can be workarounds and riddles, evading the inner critic.

Drop seven questions on your page now, as you surface from your practice. Any questions at all. There's nothing too weird or too simple or too much.

Later this week, consider coming back to answer one of the questions with a few minutes of free-writing. Maybe it's a place to begin your next writing time.

52

What part of your writing wants to REST now? Is there a story that needs space to breathe, sleep, dream?

What part of your writing wants to EXPAND now? Is there a word or image that feels connected to it?

53

What CIRCLES in the writing today?

Notice an image, word, question, or idea that seems to return, recur, or swirl closer. What is it pointing to or protecting?

(I imagine it like a killdeer protecting her nest, how she swoops and circles on the ground. What's in the nest with you?)

54

What feels light, shallow, or even
frivolous today?

Where do you sense your speaker or
yourself dabbling along the shore,
rather than diving deep?

What if you meet those lines or
sentences just as they are, without
judgement? What do you appear to be
dabbling with now as a writer?

55

Find three phrases or sentences that might belong to the world you are creating (or remembering) in this writing.

What climate or weather do you sense in them?

What atmosphere is being created?

56

Where does your writing today do, say,
or focus on something that feels true
to your way of being?

Examine this moment to notice the
techniques or creative choices at play.
Is it in first, second, or third person?
Past or present tense? Full of bold
verbs or humming with subtle
descriptions? Short, swift lines or
long, rolling sentences?

What gives this moment life and space
on the page? And does that point to
something you might be drawing from or
developing in your voice as a writer?

57

Invent five rough titles for your writing today. Even if you think you have a working title, try five new possibilities.

What does this writing <u>want</u>, <u>announce</u>, <u>demand</u>, or <u>believe</u>? Aim for titles that aren't shy about taking up space.

(It can be fun to repeat this at regular intervals with an ongoing project. Rough title lists can show how you're relating to the work or how the "big idea" changes over a series of drafts. They're a quick way to document the evolution of a piece.)

58

Where did you pull close, to examine a feeling, explain steps, or describe something in detail today?

Where did you lean away, to reflect on the bigger picture or write about a larger theme?

What's calling to you more as a writer now: the big picture or close attention?

How is your orientation making the writing stronger? How is it making the process clearer?

59

What's one thing you could bring to messy completion this week?

Something small enough to be manageable... and interesting enough to be meaningful.

A poem? The first full (however rough) draft of an essay? An important scene in your story?

60

What material feels most urgent in your practice now?

How are you meeting the urgency? Does it feel messy and uncertain, or clear and persistent? What is one way you are experimenting with urgency (or not) now?

61

What are five things you're glad you
don't have to know about right now?

How is UN-knowing showing up and
possibly aiding your practice now?

62

What was the most certain or confident choice you made while practicing today?

It might have happened on the page (e.g., a choice about where to break a line), in your mind (e.g., a choice to ignore some feedback), or in your practice (e.g., a choice to use a certain pen or sit in a certain spot).

What momentum did this choice create?

Is this a new kind of certainty for you, or is it familiar to your practice?

63

Find one line, sentence, or paragraph that lingers, pauses, or maybe even hesitates. Where does the writing slow down?

What do you notice about the material in these moments?

Is this a natural part of your pace as a writer, or is there something new showing up in it?

64

Where did you feel unprepared while writing today?

Unprepared can mean: I'm not ready.

But it can also mean: I'm open.

What are you open to now?

What is getting you ready?

65

Wherever you're at with this writing now, even if it's messy raw material, invent your own definitions (or anti-definitions... what the word is *not*) for the following words:

FINISH

COMPLETE

WHOLE

RELEASE

ENOUGH

66

What's the easiest or fastest choice you made with your practice or with this material today?

How did this choice energize you as a writer or help the material get out on the page?

What choices tend to be easy or quick for you in the creative process?

Is this something to try repeating in future writing sessions?

67

Where did you feel most impatient in
practicing today, if at all?

What does your impatience love?
What does it ignore?

Which part of you creative process
tends to get the most patience?

68

Write nine different sentences to
answer this question:

Where does the writing live,
if only for now?

69

What is the most important question
you have for the next time you write?

How would your favorite artist answer
this question?

70

What part of the writing today was just for you?

What part is yours to keep, no matter what happens next?

make your own closing practices

I hope you'll invent your own practices as
you find what's helpful and interesting to
you. It varies from writer to writer,
project to project. Here are three areas I
think of when creating closing practices:

PRACTICES FOCUSED ON MATERIAL

These can bring closer attention to
specific events and ideas happening on the
page itself. A closing practice focused on
the material can help a writer honor the
story and identify deeper work that's
unfolding with a memory or idea. This type
of closing practice can also leave an
opening for you to return—for instance,
making a list of questions you have for a
memory, to start exploring next time.
These practices grow the connection to the
material, building a bridge between writing
sessions.

PRACTICES FOCUSED ON PROCESS

These can help you locate and ground yourself in different phases of the work. Surfacing with these is a chance to notice whether a draft is nearing completion (and how it is), observing which part of the process you're enjoying or feeling challenged by, comparing the process with this draft to how other drafts have gone for you, making lists of what you're learning or asking about your voice, and so on. This type of closing practice can reveal more of your creative temperament and tendencies. I also find it helps for appreciating ways you're actually making progress, even if you thought you were spinning out or lost in the process.

PRACTICES FOCUSED ON TECHNIQUE

These are especially helpful for writers who feel like they're stagnating or getting bored with their work. With these closing practices, you focus on specific creative choices, stylistic experiments, and observations about how the writing is functioning on the page. You might make an inventory of stylistic elements showing

up in the writing (e.g., short sentences,
alliteration, second person) and choose one
to develop more consciously. The more
specific and curious you are with this
type of closing practice, the more you can
identify techniques that are natural to
you and areas for experimentation.

A parting thought on making this practice
your own: RESISTANCE is a teacher.

Wherever I feel resistance in my voice, my
process, or in the material, there's usually
a question or experiment I can turn into a
closing practice.

You don't have to know exactly why you're
resisting a technique or fighting off a
memory... it can help just to note that
it's happening, to get to know it as you
try to write through it.

about the writer

Emily Stoddard writes from a blue room
near the blue waters of Lake Michigan.
Her poetry book, Divination with a Human
Heart Attached, was released with Game
Over Books in 2023. She is a past recipient
of the Developmental Editing Fellowship in
creative nonfiction from Kenyon Review.

emilystoddard.com